#8193

A Family in Norway

A pronunciation guide for the Norwegian words and names used in this book appears on page 28.

Map on pages 4-5 is by J. Michael Roy. Front and back cover photographs courtesy of Dr. and Mrs. Johansen. Photographs on pages 16, 17, 22, 23, and 27 courtesy of Dr. and Mrs. Johansen. Photographs on pages 24 and 25 (right) courtesy of Norsk Hydro.

LIBRARY OF CONGRESS CATALOGING-IN-PUBLICATION DATA

St. John, Jetty.
  A family in Norway/Jetty St. John.
    p.   cm.
  Summary: Describes the home, school, amusements, customs, work, and day-to-day life of ten-year-old Andrea and her family living in a small village south of Oslo.
  ISBN 0-8225-1681-0 (lib. bdg.)
  1. Norway—Social life and customs—Juvenile literature.
2. Family—Norway—Juvenile literature. [1. Norway—Social life and customs. 2. Family life—Norway.] I. Title.
DL431.S78 1988   948.1—dc19   87-36783

Manufactured in the United States of America

  2 3 4 5 6 7 8 9 10 98 97 96 95 94 93 92 91

A Family in Norway

Jetty St. John

Lerner Publications Company · Minneapolis

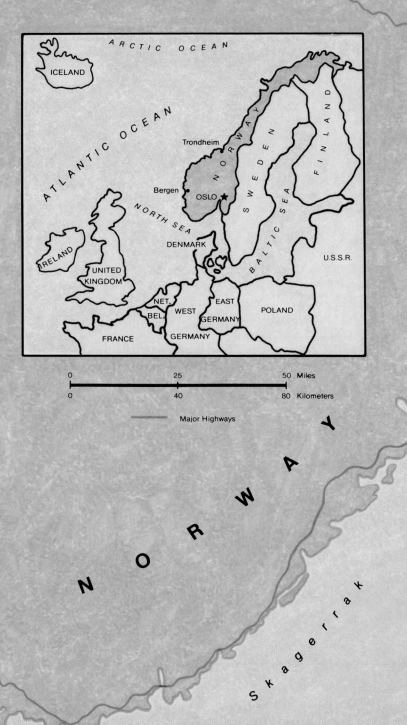

Andrea is ten years old. She lives in Drøbak, which is a small village south of Oslo, the capital of Norway. Her house looks out across a body of water called a *fjord*. Fjords are channels of water which jut inland from the sea. During the summer Andrea and her family like to eat meals on the patio, and often they see fishing boats and large passenger ships go by.

Norway, Sweden, Denmark, Finland, and Iceland together make up Scandinavia.

4

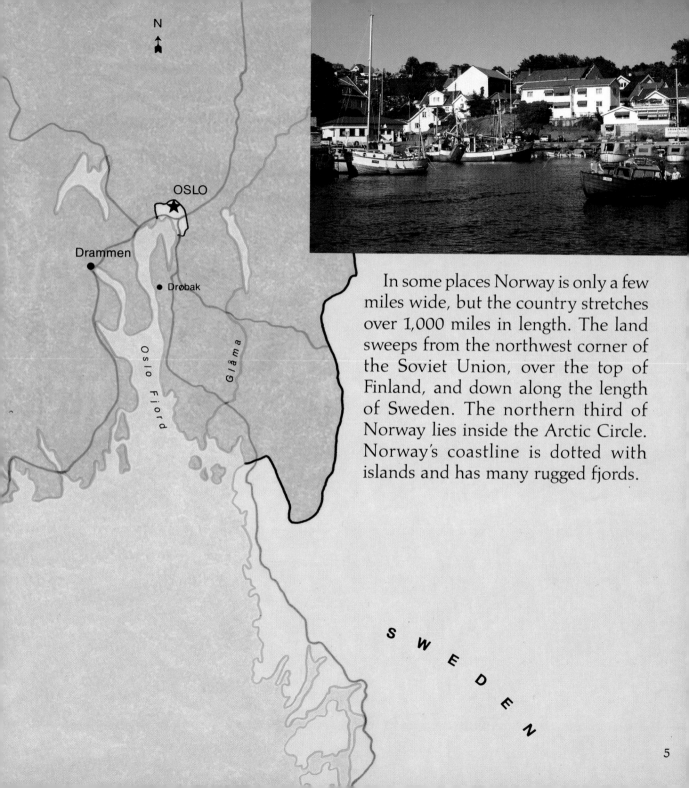

N

OSLO

Drammen

Drøbak

Oslo Fjord

Glåma

In some places Norway is only a few miles wide, but the country stretches over 1,000 miles in length. The land sweeps from the northwest corner of the Soviet Union, over the top of Finland, and down along the length of Sweden. The northern third of Norway lies inside the Arctic Circle. Norway's coastline is dotted with islands and has many rugged fjords.

SWEDEN

Andrea has two brothers. Anders is 14 years old, and Magnus is 7. During vacations they like to eat breakfast later than their parents. Their father leaves for work at 6:30 A.M. When the children have finished breakfast, they take turns doing the dishes.

When it is Anders' turn, he gets the job done as quickly as possible so he can go down to the fjord for a swim. Although Norway is very far north, the oceans and fjords are warmed by currents which come up from the Gulf Stream. The Gulf Stream is a part of the ocean, called a current, which flows in wide circular movements beginning in the Caribbean Sea. In winter the air temperature in Norway drops below zero, but the water does not freeze, and ships can still travel up the fjord to Oslo.

Andrea and Magnus help their mother with the shopping. If they have a lot to buy, they take their Volkswagen Beetle, but usually they ride their mountain bikes. Magnus prefers to walk, because he likes to climb over walls, like the one in front of their house. Sometimes he plays tricks on Andrea. If she leaves her bike outside one shop, he moves it to another.

Each day during the summer, a shrimp boat comes into the village harbor. Andrea buys some of the fresh pink shellfish for the family to eat as a late evening snack. Mrs. Johansen, Andrea's mother, takes Magnus with her to the grocery store, where there are trays of apples, strawberries, and potatoes. Fruits and vegetables are grown on the land near Norway's coastal inlets and in the mountain valleys. Small dairy farms also produce milk and cheese. Mrs. Johansen often buys soft brown goat cheese for breakfast. Most of the land in Norway is too mountainous to grow crops. Instead, acres of trees are planted for timber.

Usually Andrea sees some of her relatives in the village. Her grandmother likes to buy flowering plants, which are cultivated in greenhouses outside Drøbak. Andrea's great-grandmother lives near the harbor. She loves to sit in her garden, where she has planted colorful geraniums. Andrea visits her every day and sometimes runs errands for her.

In the afternoon Andrea's grandfather often calls to see if anyone in the family would like to go fishing with him in his wooden boat. Andrea enjoys trawling for herring, and in half an hour she has caught enough fish for the family's evening meal.

On an island opposite Drøbak is the Oscarborg Fort. During World War II the sentry on duty in the fort saw German warships surging up the fjord. The fort's commander telephoned members of Parliament in Oslo to ask what he should do. There was no time for a reply, so he ordered two cannons to be fired at the ships. A German cruiser sank, and the Norwegian king had just enough time to escape to England before more German soldiers arrived.

There is another small island across from Drøbak with a bird sanctuary on it. Grandfather waits in the boat while Andrea and her mother go ashore to collect shells. Magnus runs backwards and forwards over the stones — he says they do not hurt his feet at all.

Andrea cleans the fish she has caught, then she and her mother fry them. They also cook fresh broccoli and a dish called *pytti panna*, or "bits and pieces." They make it from potatoes, onions, and any other vegetables that happen to be in the refrigerator. Mrs. Johansen can also buy fish in the village, since small boats go out each day to catch cod and herring. Traditionally, fish were dried in villages along the shore, but today the catches are often canned or frozen and then exported to other countries. Along the coast Norway has many large fleets equipped with radar and fish detectors.

Dr. Johansen arrives home by 5:30 P.M., and he is usually hungry. Like many other Norwegians, he works through lunch and eats only a sandwich at his desk. After the evening meal he usually goes for a bike ride in the countryside to get some exercise. Anders often goes with him.

Each day Andrea's father travels to Oslo by Hovercraft. A Hovercraft is a vehicle that moves on a cushion of air over land or water. If Dr. Johansen has a special meeting, he drives to work. He is the head of the Norwegian Academy of Sciences. The Academy employs scientists to do research in medicine, zoology, law, astrophysics, and chemistry. Andrea's father oversees research projects all over the world and often travels abroad. Once every three weeks the king of Norway, Olav V, visits the Academy and talks with Dr. Johansen about the different projects.

Dr. Johansen is an archaeologist, someone who studies the remains of ancient cultures. He works with researchers at museums where Viking ships are housed. The 1,000-year-old vessels were found buried in the mud of the Oslo Fjord. Tools and weapons on board provide clues about the life of the Vikings. Vikings were Norwegian explorers who made many journeys from about A.D. 800 –1100. Dr. Johansen can learn something about these seafarers by looking at the writing on their tombstones. Vikings formed colonies in Iceland and Greenland, and it is thought that they were the first Europeans to reach North America.

During vacations Andrea often goes out walking in the mountains with her father. Many of the mountains have snow on them all year. Rivers flow down the mountains to the sea, but most of the rivers are far too cold for swimming.

Andrea's father writes books about the Bronze Age, the period between 4000 and 3000 B.C. The family sometimes drives to a place near the Swedish border two hours away from Drøbak to look at rock carvings. The carvings are at least 3,000 years old. Some of the carvings show boats that were used during the Bronze Age. People used to row the boats all the way to what are now Denmark and West Germany to get copper and tin so they could make bronze weapons, tools, and cooking utensils.

Andrea and Anders go to the elementary school in Drøbak. Now that Magnus is seven years old, he has also started school. Students go to the elementary school for nine years. Some students then attend a vocational training school, and others go to a junior college before going to a university. Andrea's favorite subject in school is geography, but she doesn't like Norwegian grammar very much.

Andrea often has homework to do. While studying, she takes a break and draws.

The school is only a five-minute walk up the road. Classes for Andrea and Anders start at 8:15 A.M. Andrea comes home at 1:00 P.M., and Anders comes back an hour later. Magnus usually has three hours of school in the morning. Mrs. Johansen prepares open sandwiches for the children to take for their lunch. They often have smoked salmon and lettuce. During the holidays their mother bakes cakes and Danish pastries for a treat.

In Drøbak there is a wooden church that was built 100 years ago. Andrea and her family go there for weddings. Most of the churches are made of timber, as are Norwegian houses. The stave churches, made of narrow strips of wood, are the oldest. They have survived since the time of the Vikings. Andrea has seen a stave church in a museum near her father's office. The inside of the church was dark, because there were no windows. The roof outside, however, was decorated with wooden tiles and carved dragon heads, which are a symbol of the Vikings.

Andrea's grandmother takes care of the family's national costumes. She has to iron them carefully because they are made of wool. The family wears the costumes at weddings and on *Syttende Mai* or 17 May, which is Constitution Day. Constitution Day is also known as Children's Day, because school children parade throughout the towns and villages of Norway on that day. Every year Andrea and Anders take part in a procession through Drøbak, each carrying a small Norwegian flag. This year Magnus will also be old enough to join them. In Oslo thousands of school children walk up the main street leading to the royal palace. King Olav V waves to them from his balcony.

For vacations, the family drives north to their *hytte* or cabin in the mountains. It takes six hours to get there. The cabin used to be part of an old farm. Inside they have bunk beds, a wooden table and chairs, and a small stove for cooking. In the summer they go hill climbing, and there is plenty of open space for horseback riding.

At Christmas and at Easter the family cross-country skis from the hytte. Andrea learned to ski as soon as she could walk. Sometimes the family also skis on the floodlit trails around Drøbak. When Andrea's father was a student, he used to take part in the national ski-jumping competition at the Holmenkollen ski jump in Oslo. Skiing is now the national sport, but people used to ski mostly as a means of transportation.

Some of the scientists who work with Dr. Johansen do research for Norsk Hydro, one of the largest power companies in Norway. It builds oil-drilling rigs in the North Sea and has developed many hydroelectric stations to generate power from mountain rivers.

Power generated from water, or hydroelectric power, produces 99 percent of the electricity needed in Norway. By using fairly cheap electricity, Norwegian industries can flourish. Some things Norwegian factories produce are aluminum, canned food, and electrical machinery.

Many people now work in industry instead of being farmers or fishermen. Most people in Norway earn enough money to live fairly well.

Each year Andrea's father goes on archaeological expeditions with his friend Thor Heyerdahl. They travel to remote parts of the world to find buried relics. The relics provide information about ancient peoples. Andrea's father tells her that they hope to find pyramids which have remained hidden for hundreds of years in South America. During their travels, Dr. Johansen and Dr. Heyerdahl sometimes go horseback riding. They enjoy going up into the mountains.

Andrea also enjoys horseback riding. She is especially fond of the sturdy, beige-colored Norwegian horse called the *fjording*. These horses are still used for work on Norwegian farms.

Andrea likes to hear about her father's travels. She hopes that one day she too will be able to go on expeditions.

Norwegian Words and Names in This Book

Andrea ahn-DRAY-ah
Anders AHND-ersh
Drøbak DRUB-ahk
fjord FEE-OR
fjording FEE-OR-ing
Holmenkollen HOHL-men-KOHL-len
hytte HIHT-teh
Johansen yo-HAHN-sen
Magnus MAHG-noos
Norsk Hydro NOHRSK HEE-droh
Olav OH-lahv
Oscarborg OHS-car-bohrg
Oslo OHSH-loh
pytti panna PIHTT-ee PAHN-neh
Syttende Mai SIHT-ten-neh MY
Thor Heyerdahl TOHR HIRE-dahl

Facts about Norway

Capital: Oslo

Language: Norwegian

The Norwegian language has two forms, Bokmål and Nynorsk, which are gradually being combined into a single form called Samnorsk.

Form of Money: krone

Area: 125,052 square miles (323,883 square kilometers)

Norway is slightly larger than the state of New Mexico.

Population: About 4,158,000

Norway has about three times as many people as New Mexico.

National Holiday: Constitution Day, May 17

NORTH
AMERICA

SOUTH
AMERICA

Norway

EUROPE

ASIA

AFRICA

AUSTRALIA

Families the World Over

Some children in foreign countries live like you do. Others live very differently. In these books, you can meet children from all over the world. You'll learn about their games and schools, their families and friends, and what it's like to grow up in a faraway land.

Lerner Publications Company, 241 First Avenue North, Minneapolis, Minnesota 55401